Praise for *Mettle*

'A stunning debut, threading land, ocean and heart together in an expansive Māori tapestry that speaks to our present, shared moment. *Mettle* is alive with ancient knowing, breathing possibilities into every line. An outstanding read.' **Leanne Betasamosake Simpson**

'This is heartbeat poetry, the kind of collection that changes the reader with salt and fire and mettle. Magnificent.' **Jazz Money**

'Mettle: of courage and grit, of pluck and resolve. This is sitting around the kitchen table, two hands smoothing out the "good" or "day to day" tablecloth with instinct and deliberation. This stunning debut is straight out nana-talk, poetic memoir, and weaving all the tiny-big things, all longing and heart and of the earth.' **Natalie Harkin**

'Poems born from that painful place between death and rebirth, telling their truth "slant", allowing reader and writer to understand how resiliency arrives gradually.' **Sandra Cisneros**

'It is rare to observe in print the diverse realities that construct the contemporary Māori diaspora. Anne-Marie's nuanced poems masterfully weave the losses, longings and joys of being Māori in Australia with the karanga (the spiritual call) that binds us to our ancestral homelands, the Hokianga in Far North Aotearoa, New Zealand.' **Maarama (Jo) Kamira**

'Anne-Marie Te Whiu's poetic voice is bright, and new. Just listen to this line: "moonstone hues bud horizon …" She brings the heightened power of spirited composition to the formally innovative structures of experimental poetics, and yet mixes that compositional dexterity with story-based memory. A filmic encounter in the Salvation Army Store after lockdown, or a vulnerable memory of a mother's asthmatic attack, bring out the emotions of connection and disconnection. As well as vividly poetic storytelling, the humour here is mordant – "i recite a karakia for my brothers / they would prefer kebabs" – and in the best spirit of a bustling, diverse Indigenous poetics it excels in the most tuneful, colloquial, "high and low" voices of another poet from Northland, Hone Tuwhare, and that most spiritual and earthy poet of the south, Keri Hulme.' **Robert Sullivan**

'I always wonder how we get through it, *it* being this settler colonial existence, and I think the answer is: play. This book plays with words in such a way that you can see through all the bullshit straight into the heart of our Indigenous futures. One where we fuck and grieve and love and joke and talk shit and howl for the world that has hurt us. Let us play, very seriously, very revolutionarily, very queerly, very Māori, let us play.' **essa may ranapiri**

'"Mettle" suggests the ingrained capacity to meet difficulty with fortitude and resilience. Te Whiu's poems generously weave this capacity into brilliantly understated pieces with seared edges. Her kupu, an ingrained rope pulled taut for us to walk upon, to feel the fear, the strain, and have the courage to continue forward. A simple resounding reminder of how to live this life.' **Aziembry Aolani**

Mettle

Anne-Marie Te Whiu is an Australian-born Māori (Te Rarawa) poet, editor, cultural producer and weaver living on unceded Wangal Country in Australia. *Mettle* is her debut poetry collection.

METTLE

ANNE-MARIE
TE WHIU

UQP

First published 2025 by University of Queensland Press
PO Box 6042, St Lucia, Queensland 4067 Australia
Reprinted 2025

University of Queensland Press (UQP) acknowledges the Traditional Owners and their custodianship of the lands on which UQP operates. We pay our respects to their Ancestors and their descendants, who continue cultural and spiritual connections to Country. We recognise their valuable contributions to Australian and global society.

uqp.com.au
reception@uqp.com.au

Cover design by Madeline Byrne, University of Queensland Press
Cover illustration by Momoe i manu ae ala atea'e Tasker
Typeset in 11.5/14 pt Adobe Garamond Pro by Post Pre-press Group, Brisbane
Printed in Australia by McPherson's Printing Group

University of Queensland Press is supported by the Queensland Government through Arts Queensland.

University of Queensland Press is assisted by the Australian Government through Creative Australia, its principal arts investment and advisory body.

A catalogue record for this book is available from the National Library of Australia.

ISBN 978 0 7022 6867 0 (pbk)
ISBN 978 0 7022 6999 8 (epdf)

University of Queensland Press uses papers that are natural, renewable and recyclable products made from wood grown in well-managed forests and other controlled sources. The logging and manufacturing processes conform to the environmental regulations of the country of origin.

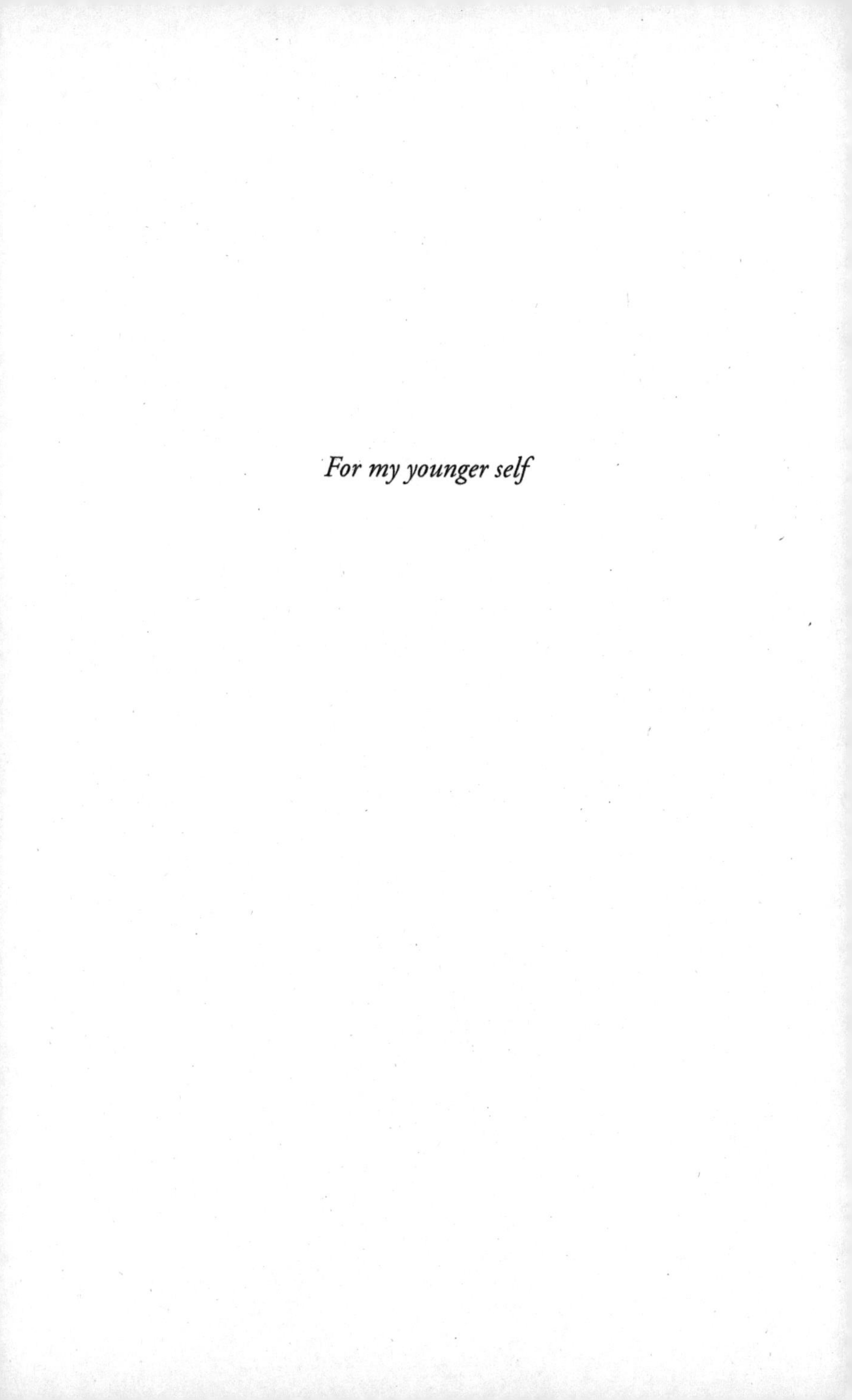

For my younger self

'Those who move with courage make the path
for those who live in fear.'

—Eve L. Ewing, *Ironheart, Vol. 1: Those With Courage*

Contents

Platinum

Fractured

Malleable

Lustrous

Mercurial

Reflective

PLATINUM

High Tide of Relationality

Ko Te Reinga toku maunga
ko Waihou te awa
ko Hokianga te moana
ko Waihou-Nui-a-Rua te marae
ko Waimirirangi te whare tupuna
ko Te Rarawa tōku iwi
ko Te Waekoi tōku hapū
ko Anne-Marie Te Whiu tōku ingoa

my pepeha
my descent profile
opens you and me up to the possibility
of blood connection and situates us in relation
to the landmarks where my bones belong

one of the starting points
between you and me
is here on this page
I'll hold on
to one end
of a line
you the other
let's pull the rope tight
learn from the tension
build from the slack

A Returning

Hokianga blue blood
ferry my waka
reggae & chur bro
in the front seats
fish & chips soggy
on the dash

Kohukohu calls me close
thick morning mist rises
wild pigs draped over tray-back
Panguru stretches the afternoon

roads made of gravelled potholes
hongi one hundred times on the marae
dawn stars open up Lower Waihou
two wild horses flare their nostrils
hooves stub dirt poi tails twist

Te Reinga asks:
Where have you been?

I lower my eyes
Aroha mai, it has taken so long

Te Puna O Te Ao Marama

ancient
light

tide
breathing

Koutu boulders
Tāne Mahuta's shoulders

how many taniwha
kauri logs & orca & ships

have you carried?

Today the harbour, like the Reformation itself, stands between Protestant and Catholic.

ohhhhh Wikipedia

car ferry   to Kohukohu
your bar crossed
flooded roads   to Panguru

waterlogged waka
time will tell
we are shipwrecked

It was this encroachment of British colonial laws over Māori autonomy that instigated an armed protest, the response to which became known as the Dog Tax War.

your dark sky sanctuary
your three lashed estuaries

your dunes hold me
close

my bones
are yours

te reo & i

I HAVE NO IDEA WHAT YOU ARE SAYING

i exist here

I know exactly what you are saying

i exist here

I HAVE NO IDEA WHAT YOU ARE SAYING

i exist here

I know exactly what you are saying

i exist here

I HAVE NO IDEA WHAT YOU ARE SAYING

i exist here

I know exactly what you are saying

i exist here

I HAVE NO IDEA WHAT YOU ARE SAYING

i exist here

I know exactly what you are saying

Angled

when the palm of the day

kisses the shoulder of dusk

moonstone hues bud horizon

blue whales draw their eyes up

glancing mottled sea surface

it is not so much the loss of light

nor the rising arc of sirius star

it is more an ancient breeze

first warmed by sun eons ago

then circled around sideways rain

blanketed in tomorrow

the ache of our ancestors

restrained by rusted anchor

fresh and salt water

carry all that is good

arctic char catches currents

bait waits to be hooked

stunned tails turn

to face

their hunter

Timeless

I own plenty of watches

but am always running late

they are draped from a hook

above precious paraphernalia

none of them tick-tock

their hands

frozen in a moment

I cannot seem to let them go

if I throw them out

I am tossing away time

I choose to treasure them

and instead look to sun and stars

to guide me

their boundless hands reach out

holding me

letting me know

where and how and why

I am here

FRACTURED

də'mɛstɪk

police car in driveway
bed unmade since yesterday
blue and red lights up the street
not far to fall
Christmas-induced abuse
flee home at midnight
leave behind kids and plants to be watered
able to walk but not think
dog hiding in the garage
empty cheque-book empty tank
from suburb to city to sanctuary
soil to cement
each body is its own
owned by your husband, the church, the government
don't pack the dirty dishes
no more knocks at the door
the coolest room in the house is the bathroom
jealousy overflows in the kitchen
still wearing wedding rings
falling in lust so young
with a man from afar
serve your husband not the house
set off the fire alarms in the kitchen
wear the pearls he bought you
spill gravy on your dress
he will sit at the head of the table
you will take your place to the left
be grateful for the blender, microwave and mixer
don't touch the paperwork he brings home

the iron keeps his collars hard
you will not be believed
you own unwashed washing
turn up the transistor
smile at his parents
never know his origins
vacuum while he mows
calculate your escape on Sundays after mass
every day repeat

Dark as Last Night

telephone rings loud
I leave home
looking like someone
you might want
feel for ridges
keys in pocket
rib cage against
lining of coat
I catch a tram
direct to your apartment
front door to grey carpet
sticky handrail to staircase
this roof does not shelter me
walls wail
shoulders ripe
ready to be used
back to the bruise

hood/ie

a brief visit is best
i plan my departure upon arrival
four flights of stairs lead to their place
a reinvented six-pack apartment block

they hear my footsteps pre-empt my knock
front door heavily locked freed by clean-cut keys

flyscreen flicked to release held open by pressure pump
my youngest brother greets me, his swollen stomach and
unshaven grin

shoes off – socks on
family photos hang from when we Once Were
a hundred DVDs stick tightly together on a bookshelf
Mum's ashes take pride of place
a pyramid of pre-rolled cigarettes waits patiently

my other brother remains seated holding TV remote
what have you got under that hoodie?

he is propped up by the only softness he knows now
crevices of leather lounge he sinks into
his tongue is loose with weapons
counting cars – switching channels – clicking dials
i ask him how he is doing and what he's been up to
he tells me the smoke alarm batteries need to be changed

i pull back a heavy light-out curtain
hoping to find the sun but instead blinds

Blood Brothers

i recite a karakia for my brothers
they would prefer i bring kebabs

i tell them about the Hokianga
they tell me about their bills

i explain tangata whenua
they turn up the TV

i dream of Tāne Mahuta
they roll a cigarette

i summon the names of our ancestors
they take their medication

i miss our marae
they put out the bins

Full of Grace

grade five finished
school holidays adrenaline
it was christmas eve
a packed house
thurible smoked us out

i played mary
towering over joseph
he had the blondest hair
and bluest eyes
other kids dressed
as sheep
as oxen
do not forget the donkey

three wise men
from grade four
flanked the manger
while
mum and dad
brought their best show

from fighting at home
to smiles and wedding rings
my three brothers
a tryptic of altar boys
serving under the cross

the itch of the veil
the sting of the salt
hot on my cheek
the congregation sang

Come to the water
You who are thirsty

jesus cradled in my arms
the only baby I've ever had

How to Solve a Rubik's Cube

We were four and the Ku's were six. Together we ten kids easily made two teams for games. Across the road was Stephen and his sister, Alison, who were only allowed to play on the streets on weekends. I hated Kevin Holder. He lived five houses along, near the bend in the road. Kevin would stand at the top of his steep driveway, staring, glaring, swearing. The bully. Our neighbours on one side had a lonely dog and no kids. When footballs ended up in their backyard my oldest brother would hoist himself over the fence and sprint to the precious object to retrieve it silently, triumphantly. Our fence stretched beyond our anguish, beyond our brick home, beyond the quarrels and shouting and silence and belting. Beyond the confusion, the pressure, the cracks and blood, which refused to flow. The Perrys, our neighbours on the other side, were Mum's favourites. They had a golden retriever we all loved, and a coveted pool we loved even more. The Perrys were kind. We could swim for hours on stinking-hot days. They would hear the fighting at night and know that Mum needed a break. My brothers and I would shout 'Marco / Polo' at each other, followed by bombs in the deep end. My head filled with bubbled silence. <END>

creepy crawly

suburban shark

chlorinated skin

blotched red eyes

pruned fingers

running

on hot wet

slippery cement

I wore my rollerskates more than my shoes
my brothers and I put two skateboards side by side
and would catamaran down St Marks Avenue
down to the BMX track by the creek
picking mulberries and silkworms
I wore togs and volleys all day
sometimes my eldest brother
would let me wear his old pink, fluorescent Okanuis
we traded footy cards
chalked handball squares on bitumen
games interrupted by 'CAR!'
cicadas were my trophy
we woke at 3 am to spot Halley's Comet
waited for weeks to watch *Thriller* on TV
laid flattened cardboard boxes down in the garage
on top of leaked car oil
and did bad breakdance

One summer killed our car. Steam shot out of the bonnet
as Mum's tears fell. She had an asthma attack on the side
of the road; two guys with surfboards on their roof-racks
pulled over. One drove her to the hospital. The other stayed
with us. He fake-smiled and told us everything would
be alright. I knew it wouldn't.

We piled into the car every Sunday morning
Dad would smoke his ciggies with the windows barely down
The Doobie Brothers sang us to mass

MALLEABLE

The Politics of Eggs

my account says
you will not buy
free range
organic
pasture-raised
happy
eggs

my account says
you will buy
cage eggs

I look around
my apartment
wondering if I
could sneak in
four or five chickens
could I set them up
in my bathroom
lay eggs in the tub?

Mistaken Identity in the Pie Shop

The lady behind the counter sees me and looks at me a little too long.
She makes a shape with her eyes and mouth. It makes me think something is wrong.
She flicks her chin at me and says:

Yuuaaa avvaaa sistaa?!
yuuaa avvaaa sistaa
sheeeea livaaaa in da baaaaiiiiiy.

She points, over her right shoulder.
What is she talking about? Does she mean this bay?
Island Bay?
I'm sure there's a couple of other bays in Wellington.

Yuuaa sistaaaaa
sheeaaa Francescaaa
myaa friendaaa
we havaava daa coffeee together aaahh!

Her face is beaming.
She looks at me like I'm a little bit stupid and that surely pennies will drop.
That finally I'll realise who she is, who I am and how Francesca connects us.

'I have three brothers,' I say.
I want a steak & cheese.
I want to make a quick exit.

Naaaahhh
yuuuuaaaa!

She really looks at me.
I feel like she's going to come from behind the counter and inspect me up close.
Her eyes start to sparkle. Her eyelashes might take flight.
She holds her hands out like a sculptor and cups them around my face.
Awwww
yuuuaa lookaa daa saaama.

'I get this a lot,' I say, explaining that she's not the first person I've met who is absolutely convinced that I am someone they know.

I think back to the long list of past

Italian
Turkish
Chinese
Samoan
Inuit
Native American
Iranian
Taiwanese
Spanish
French
Egyptian

eventually

Māori

She wipes her hands on a tea towel tucked into her front,
looks at the pie cabinet and says:

'Septaa sheeaaea muchaaa slimma danna yuuu!

Salvation Army

Shopping Centre Formation

One of the worst things about lockdown was the
  Salvation Army closed
It is the one shop in the world that I truly love being inside
Generally, I find that shops suck
Now that the Salvos have reopened
I am returning
Maybe too regularly these days
Like I'm making up for all those lost weeks
When I stalked the pull-down roller door
Re-reading the sticky-taped notice

WE ARE CLOSED DUE TO COVID-19
AND WILL REOPEN WHEN IT IS SAFE

There is no time in Salvos

I imagine what my morning coffee will taste like
In this gorgeous handmade ceramic mug
With an RL engraved at the base
It is $1.50
I am going to give this mug
A good life

Today a person mostly wearing purple
Gently pushing a walking frame
Inspected the customers browsing
More than any of the glorious things for sale

I was knee-deep in the softest of 70s fabrics
When she approached
Speaking not to me
But around me
Luring me in
Waiting for my eyes to meet hers

She told me all about:
~ her broken arm
~ a junkie had knocked her over
~ she'd been up at the courts
~ she knew him
~ so did the courts
~ the university was making synthetic drugs for the police
~ they were selling the drugs and cashing in on the extra arrests
~ she survived living with a nazi
~ she married god recently
~ he was her real husband
~ she felt a little dizzy

'There's a movie about my life and you can download it for free on the YouTube.
It's called *Hostage*, and they made millions off that film, and I made nothing. But you can still watch it.'

'I will! What's your name?'

'Christine.'

she smiled back at me
through stained, chipped teeth

Sauria

sweat
clung
to
your
shiny
head

skin
peeled
from
the
lids
of
your
azure
eyes

sinking
slithering
slough

I called the snake catcher

when she finally arrived
she caught you
and held you by the head

your jaw wide open
silently screaming

she said she had never
seen one
like you before
and advised
I leave you
to the elements

Electric Fence

effective solution
exclusion zone
energy shunt
permanent high
tensile system
wired control
retrofitted mania
metal teeth

gnaw

crown your anger
                                        let go
                                                            let go
                                                                                let go
chest inflates in the shirt I bought him
repressed calves cling to jeans
AC voltage type mood swings
tetanus tethered memories
barbed cables break
galvanised ego exposed
no room for time
Ōturu knows the season
eye contact is dangerous
keep lashes low

key left on deck
open front door
collect the dog

her paws stay close
when she is with me
stick does not throw
chew is not bitten

he (apparently)   accommodates
i (apparently)   conflate
he (apparently)   regulates
i (apparently)   mimic
he
i
he
i
blahhhblahhhblahhh

select   your   mask
block   ugly   email
bar   the   banter
scrape   shallow   memory
undercooked   man   overboard
his   sea/e-(ing)   legs
left   at   sure line
remember   a   way
to   return   to

myself

tomorrow he will be
~~different~~ the same
tomorrow he will be
~~different~~ the same
tomorrow he will be
~~different~~ the same

i fool myself into thinking that change is inevitable
but
he
is
the
same
same as he ever was
same as he
same as he
same same

i turn
the page
plug in
wait for
signal my
main line
is grounded

Stay the Line

When I stay inside the line
edges spiral out
insides curdle
watch your back
you never know

When I stand behind the line
I rub it out
chalk in the rain
nothing to see here
blank stares for miles

When I read between the lines
rainbow sings to greys
a yesterday sky
each cloud louder than the last
forever blue

When I get in line
I am usually at the back
trying to tear off
to a forest or an ocean or a book
final page reveals all

When I toe the line
I last one minute
sixty second escape plan
which takes a lifetime
to find

When I hold the line
I peel back and sing forward
notes hit warm breeze
no low necks here
grief aired with love

When I cross the line
we meet in the shallows
foam foliates face
seaweed then wave
each body floats

LUSTROUS

Land as Body

I was already here
following my seasons
tracing each leaf
bark peeling
fingering my ravine

you and your rudder
did not discover me
I know my winds
I know my true north
I know these waters

your anchor
is not
welcome here

Smells Like Colonial Spirit

always a man next door
clearing his throat
stripping the land
tightening his belt
stroking his beard
he has a vision
for an extension
for development
a need to renovate
a push to reshape
a man-spread
his patch of turf
each metre controlled
measurements defined
as right as nails
corners hardened
bricks hold down plans
planks of foreign wood delivered
raising his leg
marking his territory
making his man shed

I will burn it down
before first light
and spread the ashes
in the car park

Missionary Position

in the race to assimilate
the long white cloud
the weather was turned
flat on her back
stretched wide open
ancient brown thighs
harbour dunes chapped
against whakapapa
tīpuna channelled
hold your line
in the name of the father
carry your blood
hongi the holy spirit
translate a bible
whipped for the reo
stimulated trade
lusted for kauri
draped in gold crosses
coming in colonial peace
blankets for acres

piece by piece

under cover

under robes

the deed was done

reading waves

oh
hey
are
you
looking
down?
what do you see?
is white water foaming?
swirling at your feet and ankles?
are clear shallows drawing you in?
did you check the tide times before leaving home?
bite your lip
return your mouth
to familiar
sounds
return
again
again
again

i
n
f
i
n
i
t
e

c rest upon curl
yearning
rip curl
rip
it

good now we can shred choose your moon she will mother
you stare through the eye of the barrel which dawning did
you vote for or maybe you could not accept the degree
of spaciousness the politics of these waters is rough apex
creatures thrive hunt in packs time to say goodbye to all you
once knew enter the impact zone with aroha and grace you
will find out who you really are and who they are not loosen
your grip and soften your brow follow your heart to a peak
greed is not welcome here lap ahead with ease please off your
knees little shoulder shrugs finally ready to face your old fears

MERCURIAL

Pash

i slid in
so that
your sides
were curled to
mine

softly leant on
hard pew
whispered breath
arched neck
longest hour

cupped hands
waiting
to feel for
your every
crevice

Love Letter to Keri Hulme

– for essa

17 Jenner Road
Beachville
Nelson 7010

30 March 1984

Kia ora Keri,

I've just walked in. The bus trip home was pretty awful.

I sat behind a couple who were silent-fighting the whole way.
I guess that was better than them loud-arguing.
The bus got a flat tyre in Westport, so we were delayed by
about an hour.

All of this made the ache of leaving you even more difficult.
I will be brief as I know you're in the middle of such
important writing.
There are two things I had to share with you.

Firstly, to thank you for opening your whare to me.
A weekend I will remember for returning to myself and
being with you.
I smell of you – tobacco and whitebait and beer sing on
my skin.
I loved every minute with you, in your place, at your pace.

And secondly, I wanted to let you know,
I read the part of *The Bone People* draft manuscript you shared with me, on the bus.
I had to stop about halfway through because of motion sickness.
I'll devour the other half tonight in bed.

K, it is full of contradictions – my favourite style of writing. And people.

It is sparse and full all at once
shapeless and totally contained
wild and almost unkept
yet still and perfect
directive and open
sweet and wild

Your words clip my ears and run their hands through my hair.
Ngaa mihi e hoa for sharing your mahi with me in this way.
My door is open. Please do visit me soon if you can.

Always,
Ani

I Am an Oyster

~ for them

shuck me in my bed of porcelain sheets

brackish

reef

undone

longing to be taken in one fell swoop

whole

mouth

salt

eat me while the tide is high

Dog Exclusive

I used to be
a dog-exclusive girl
until this morning
when under the bridge I met you
tiger
thick paws
slow tail
a body you let me pat
curled around my ankles
a seasoned sun seeker
you hunted the light
purring prancing preying
you let me
get in behind your ears
stroke your side
back arched
one of my steps were 6 of yours
you followed me
so that we were together
until the end of the alley

then you bit me

Chosen

-for Tessa

Inside my puku dwells a whānau of wrestlers
whose shoulders for boulders wrap with
pretty punch force twisting knots
into black butterflies

They are my
blood and flesh
I will try
to eat with them tomorrow
before or after an eruption
of old and new wounds

Today my friends
are cushions
whose eyes for oceans
see me through
high tide
listening and holding
that which mine own
cannot carry

A Bibliography of a Weave

this morning i woke
with another weaving hangover
it reached 3 am and 3 baskets were full
their happy centres staring back at me
strong to the core
able to hold everything that was to come
I cupped each one in both hands
slowly inspecting their curves
the way the raffia tucked in
trimming inflorescence
satisfaction of editing
a weave

thumb callused
flecked fibres cover my lap
scissors lost under a pillow or rug
tomorrow I will need to scour
suburban streets for more fibres
eyes to the skies
scanning for bangalow palms
their sheath beds asleep
feeling for wind
hoping for heavy rain
that will deliver branches
to the earth's floor

conjure

take two tablespoons of quicksand with food
preferably in the morning
it will help you see that the sun and fire are one

fill a bottle with ocean water
heat until boiled
allow to cool then pour it over your attitude

collect six ripened stars
swallow them whole at dusk
dance for a month after ingestion

drain your nightmares
keep them in an airtight jar
crack glass against red brick

find a feather
wrap it in bark
place under your pillow
for courage

Beginnings of an interrogation of the text

OLD NEW ZEALAND: A Tale of the Good Old Times
By a Pakeha Maori Edited by F. E. Manning,
Whitcombe and Tombs Limited, Auckland.

I step inside but the outside moves with me
the deeper I go the more I know there are no partitions
humidity and rain finally reel me in
I scan in and slide my way to the inside of another inside
tables inched together with doubt-raising gaps

in the same way
that
different fonts
grouped together
can make
you feel
uneasy

a staff member smiles then quickly looks away
I pull a chair heavy on the polished cement floor
tuck in
knees curled close
commit my mind to laptop trenches

I open a book
the one borrowed
years ago
you know what it is like

it travelled a long way
smuggled out
hard cover looks soft now
ready to
face the music

kanohi ki te kanohi
my flammable eyes survey brazen li~~es~~nes
the curved recesses of my forty-seven years
fingers flick through moth-wing dusty pages
some books look like bibles in disguise

I breathe in historical odour
the archive of me meets the archive of him
my brown blood on simmer
pages of the book come away from the lumbar spine
twisted history fails the polygraph

After the Fire

is a house still a house when the ceiling has collapsed?
it won't shelter you but the walls will do the dividing
between the business of outside and inside
looking up you will only see
paperbark and powerlines

lie s c a t t e r e d

roof
is
a
f l o o r

That In	**Words Feel My**	**Good Mouth**
Free	Free	Palestine
Speak	Your	Truth
Always	Will	Be
Come	Here	Now
Pass	The	Salt
My	Best	Friend
Nothing	Stays	Permanent
Get	Some	Sleep
Please	Forgive	Me

Grief	Is	Tidal
Zip	Me	Up
Pick	Your	Battles
Tears	Are	Healing
I	Love	You

Further than Jonah

'Mostly I just thought it was a really funny character'

my ears were the first to leave
heading off without packing anything
lobes tired of hanging on waiting
to hear something different
tired of listening to
the same old
same old

'I think I'm pretty brave with putting myself out there and looking stupid and doing things that are potentially offensive'

My eyes saw my ears take off
saw how easy it could be
without a slight or doubt in sight
to not have to watch
over and over
the same old
same old

'It's kind of funny that there's only certain races that it's an issue'

My hands grew tired of holding on
reaching out for tomorrow
nails bitten to the quick
by my anxious mind
palms furious
the same old
same old

'I've already gone far enough with the blackface thing – I can't go much further'

The last things to leave were my feet
my heart my mouth my wairua
stuck around keeping my brown skin
good company
it will take time for
the new old
new old

Gregorian Time

did you try restarting?
you are on mute
you are frozen

gel sanitiser
rub hands

are you working from home?
wash your mouth out
watch your step

get tested
self-isolation

is your internet strong?
binge *The Wire*
back to bed

hospitalised cases
covid kilos

have you signed in?
your eyes
your mask

intimate pandemic
soft toilet paper

do you have symptoms?
negative is positive
stay at home

Press esc to exit full screen

" shift to thrive
" delete to dive
" caps lock to grow
" return to open
" tab to swallow
" control to silence
" option to listen
" command to birth

before alphabets
and prisons
before nouns
and indifference
there were relationships

the domination dogma
lay dormant
no up or down
only a matrix
of oneness

come full circle
build a small
constellation of people
gather fires close
exhale and remember
how to belong

REFLECTIVE

for•te

my tattoos and
half sunset fringe
open lined eyes
drumkit lips
draw you to my
red velvet throne
all our whanau
have that same
laughter crink
in our nose
we sing before
we fight
we love before
we run
we never lock
the front door

I will look you
straight in the heart
of stories told
from the head of a table
like my Māmā did
and her Māmā before
sip slowly sip good
it stays chilled
hoodie cups my hair
my hands are a chorus
guiding us forward
take your time
slay blessed queen
smile hoops swoop
tell me
what are we made of?

A Chant Guide to One-foot-in-front-of-the-other or The Five Vertical Zones of the Ocean's Water Column

Sunlight Zone > epipelagic <
step towards moonrise
compass has no place
constellations harmonise
'I feel like I'm in a movie'
may well be said

Twilight Zone > mesopelagic <
dilated dark days
but still able to smile
mana wrapped tight
albatross feathers waterproof fears
home is double-hulled

Midnight Zone > bathypelagic <
prime rips usher sunset orange to reds
halo fluoro pink to quantum quartz black
nettle kawakawa myrtle
crush to tincture
face yourself

Abyssal Zone

> abyssopelagic <
shells have mouths
rocks have eyes
shovels are hands
clocks know nothing
a time of torture and trickery

Hadal Zone

> trenches <
the first drumbeat was a heart
still the wind howls
rubble of last breaths
it is a privilege
to grieve

(Two of) the Bodies I Have Found

I. WAYNE

Instructions

find a notebook
open to a blank page in the notebook
tear the blank page out of that notebook
using your right hand scrunch that paper
using your right hand throw that paper to the ground
find a pen
using your left hand throw the pen in the direction of
  the paper
imagine the paper is a body and the pen is a needle

Finding Him

I arrived home having been out with friends at the pub. I shared a house with three people and had guessed I was home alone because there were no lights on. Cold and quiet at 11.30 pm. I made my way up to the lounge room and turned on the TV. Started to watch *Rage*. A couple of minutes later the electric alarm clock in Wayne's room started beeping. He worked night shifts as a shelf-filler at Coles and would often sleep through the alarm. I knew this relentless beeping was not unusual. Soon the telephone rang. Wayne's manager from his work asking to speak with him. I knocked on Wayne's door, which was slightly ajar. I pushed it open gently. His heartbeat, gone.

II. NANNA

I know you're busy
I'm sorry it's late
I know you saw her on the weekend
I know you have an early start tomorrow
I know she sometimes doesn't hear the phone
I called her 10 times today and it rang out
Do you think you could drive to Wynnum and check if she's alright?

10 pm autumn lights deceptive
Draw you in and you think you're there
But you've got much further to go
Night vision no good
Gut instinct on
That feeling of a downhill road
But really, it's flat

Past East Brisbane Bowling Club
Past that bit where you can see to New Farm Park
Past the shops at Morningside
Past the Macca's at Cannon Hill
Past the curve of Hemmant Cemetery
Past the lonely netball courts
Past the overgrown football grounds

Low bridge railway tracks
Duck my head in the car
Why is it called Bride Street?
Park outside her unit and look up
Bedroom lamp on
Lace curtains hanging still

Turn the ignition off

Fumble for spare key
Silent salty Wynnum air
Inviting spirits to pass
Streetlight goes out
Adrenaline kicks in
Cold hands colder cheeks
More stairs than usual to her front door

Nanna, Nanna, it's me, are you alright?
Nanna! Where are you?
Straight to her room
Body facedown
Phlegm from mouth
Blood from cheek
Nanna in her nightie
So tiny in death

the sun'll come out

deepcore.detail.energy.frequency.self.present.
world.circadian.rhythms.opposite.algorithms
.distributed.corporation.creative.trouble.pain
ting.cent.reject.abandon.shift.desperately.poi
nt.life.culture.every.day.natural.elements.dire
ct.saltwater.immerse.body.calm.physcially.sur
render.control.everything.allow.hold.physical
.sleep.time.guided.dreaming.lucidity.deep.co
nsciousness.messages.guides.ask.receive.direc
tion.ancestral.still.time.trees.forest.clear.decis
ion.wind.forceful.lean.slight.direction.conne
ction.intelligence.surrounds.tapestry.feels.for
ce.interwoven.dynamic.connects.guide.struc
tures.governs.universe.harmony.challenges.gr
ow.plan.god.over.it.align.

Our Mums

– for Afatasi the Artist and Momoe i manu ae ala atea'e Tasker

when our mums met
they left us
no patience
they went straight to church
and sat near the aisle
they ate the bread of christ
with their hands out
amen

my mum would invite your mum over
to eat seafood at christmas time
they would eat mussels and lobsters
ocean people eating ocean food
it was a feast
the leftover taro from the night before
sliced thin
and fried up for breakfast

my mum would invite your mum
to bingo
there would be
a situation
our mums would bark out orders
we would know our mums
we know all the mums

fresh font

Garamond me good
shyness sleeps sweeps seeps
        remember?
        remember when –
                        in front of all of my friends absolute
                        100% rejection

swirling mirror ball
the carvings in the McDonald's at Māngere are crazy
I had a whole photoshoot there
between big macs and fries and a [white] cheese suprem[acy]
do you know Beyonce?
do you know The Spice Girls?
yeah man
I see them on the bus

here's a story of a lovely of a lovely
Marcia Marcia Marcia

        okay blue eyeshadow
           I see you blue eyeshadow
                       yes
                              yes side pony
                                     ride on pony

                                     show pony

                                     I'm telling you
                                     hair like mine is policed

I am the only one the one
and only
Samoan Punk Singer
Singing Punk Samoan
I keep the beat
I am the beat
we beat
the beat
DIY disco realness
I'm a regular schmegular person just trying to get by
Blak & Brown Babies have been dying at the hands of white
doctors
targeted in the birthing room
I'm tying the past
thepresentandthefuture
I never can say goodbye

MIND YOUR BUSINESS – PERIOD

Time 4 A Triptych (excerpt)

I want to get my dreams back

I am gliding. It is dark and light at the same time. It is from a time before and it is a time to come. At once it is the evening, then the sky is blush-pink and my body fly-runs through above a corridor of majestic eucalypt trees. When my feet touch the earth, I am weightless. I prefer the sensation of flying, so I glide decide to fly again. People see me flying in the air and don't bat an eyelid. I am neither here nor there, yet I feel more myself than I ever have.

Dreams are very much the act of listening

There are 12 whare in a circle with one main larger structure in the middle. The location is the Hokianga. They are all made of the most beautiful wood. Friends, travellers, musicians and visitors stay in the 12 buildings. The centre structure has a bar and kitchen downstairs with a ladder set of stairs you climb up to get to an area where performances happen. The place is packed. Music is playing. The floorboards are throbbing with love and energy.

Anything can mean anything to me

I am handwashing clothes in a freezing cold awa. My hands
can barely clean them because of how cold the water is.
I breathe out and see the exhale of thick, cloudy air in front
of me. I am at the bottom of a very steep hill. I look up and
see a shack with a dim light on. Inside, I know there is
a man polishing his shoes. I am scared but determined.
I know he does not know this land like I do.

Lion's Honey – a Reader's Moments

the train pulls into martin place
wind and city move around me
i lean towards pillared gallery
feel for friday at the sandstone entry
visitors cloak bags
find a frame to hold them
security click and count
fluorescent light casts no doubt
shadows caught on polished floors
no cracks in these walls

four flights of stairs
lead me to us
our nook
thursday's imprint still there
on the green chair
sheepskin weaves us together
our seven shelves slowly swell
every page turned
books become time
holding the line

he approaches to stare
she observes from afar
they photograph the moment
and ask why i am there

i remember
each spine
sentences underlined
titles hold tight
stories told right
memories hold light

honey

you were here before me
and you will follow me
until we are read

A Countdown

It's 11.24 pm

A deck of cards arrived about 2 months ago from Porirua
They are not tarot or angel or inspirational
They're Manawa Ora cards and they come with beautiful
  tikanga instructions

It's New Year's Eve, fast approaching 2021
My apartment block is silent – I think I'm the only one
  left awake

Outside I hear muscle cars stretching themselves in the
  distant streets, seeing how far petrol will push them
Inside I hear the oversized hanging kitsch watch-clock
  ticks when it wants to, each hand trying to move closer
  to the other, but they never meet
The fridge hums and jazzes along
It's nearly midnight

My body holds rolls
Hands know the way
My hips ache and glance my back
My flesh feels closer to fifty than ever
11.30 pm

Today I swam in a cobalt ocean with my dog
She leapt into the shallows, addicted to the sticks I threw,
  unable to stop herself
It was just us and the surfers

Fresh rain fell

It's 11.37 pm now
Thoughts dive while my thighs marinate in shame and exhaustion

11.38 pm
Time for a reading from the pack

Pull 3 –

Card 1
Reconnect
Card 2
Tohu

Card 3
Whanaungatanga

11.44 pm
These cards sing me a lullaby

11.47 pm
Fridge buzzes

Breathe in
Breathe out
Nearly āpōpō

11.58 pm
11.59 pm

Fireworks sound like gunshots tonight

Pulse

every
26
seconds
Papatūānuku
releases
a
tiny
seismic
rumble
that
ripples
out
searching
for
a
harmony
it
is
the
heart
beat
of
our
ancestors

Notes and Acknowledgements

Many thanks to those who have supported these poems and previously published them, either in differing iterations or the same.

'A Returning' appeared in *Fast Fibres Poetry 6*, edited by Piet Nieuwland and Olivia Macassey, Fast Fibres Poetry Collective, Whangārei Aotearoa/New Zealand, August 2019.

'te reo & i' appeared in *Awa Wahine: Taha Hinengaro … Mind*, Awawahine.com, Whangārei Aotearoa/New Zealand, 15 June 2020.

'Angled' appeared in *Pratik: Fire and Rain*, issue 1, edited by Sally Breen, Jennifer McKenzie and Yuyutsi Sharma, Nirala Publications and Asia Pacific Writers and Translators (APWT), New Delhi, January 2023.

'də'mɛstɪk' appeared in *Cordite 89: Domestic*, Cordite Poetry Review, edited by Natalie Harkin, Castlemaine, February 2019; *Australian Poetry Anthology: Volume 7*, edited by Yvette Holt and Magan Magan, Australian Poetry, April 2019.

'Dark as Last Night' appeared in *Women of Words: 2019–2021*, edited by Janette Hoppe, Puncher & Wattmann, Newcastle, 2022; gifted to Tony Birch for the title of his short story collection *Dark as Last Night*, UQP, Brisbane, 2021.

'hood/ie' appeared in *Sport 47*, edited by Tayi Tibble, Fergus Barrowman and Victoria University Press, Wellington, November 2019.

‘Blood Brothers’ appeared in *Ora Nui: Māori Literary Journal: New Zealand and Taiwan Special Edition*, issue 4, Anton Blank, Whangārei Aotearoa/New Zealand, April 2021.

‘Full of Grace’ appeared in *Pratik: Fire and Rain*, issue 1, edited by Sally Breen, Jennifer McKenzie and Yuyutsi Sharma, Nirala Publications and Asia Pacific Writers and Translators (APWT), New Delhi, January 2023.

‘Mistaken Identity in the Pie Shop’ appeared in *Ora Nui: Māori Literary Journal: New Zealand and Taiwan Special Edition*, issue 4, Anton Blank, Whangārei Aotearoa/New Zealand, April 2021.

‘Salvation Army’ appeared in *Rabbit: A journal for non-fiction poetry: Form*, issue 32, RMIT University and non/fictionLAB, Melbourne, April 2021.

‘Smells Like Colonial Spirit’ appeared in *Tupuranga Journal: Tahi*, issue 1, Whangārei Aotearoa/New Zealand, April 2020.

‘Missionary Position’ appeared in *No Other Place to Stand: An Anthology of Climate Change Poetry from Aotearoa New Zealand*, edited by Jordan Hamel, Rebecca Hawkes, Erik Kennedy and essa ranapiri, Auckland University Press, 2022.

‘reading waves’ appeared in ‘A tide is a very long wave’ (exhibition), curated by Sarah Hibbs, SYRUP Contemporary, Marrickville, August 2024.

‘Love Letter to Keri Hulme’ appeared in *Kupa Toi Takataapui: For Keri Hulme*, issue 1, Takataapui Literary Journal, Aotearoa/New Zealand, 2023.

'I Am an Oyster' appeared in *Unyoked Anthology; Tupuranga Journal*, Aotearoa New Zealand, April 2020.

'Dog Exclusive' appeared in *IA Literary Journal: Volume One 2.0*, Aotearoa/New Zealand, June 2020 <https://ialiteraryjournal.wixsite.com/mysite/volume-one-2-0>.

'A Bibliography of a Weave' appeared in *UnMagazine: (A collection of annotated bibliographies vol. 1)*, issue 16.1, edited by D Harling and Hilary Thurlow, un Projects, Melbourne, June 2022.

'Further than Jonah' appeared in *Cordite 100: Brownface*, edited by Winnie Dunn, Cordite Poetry Review, Castelmaine, February 2021. This poem uses extracts from an interview with Chris Lilley by Emily Orley that appeared in 'The Brownface Controversy Surrounding "Jonah from Tonga"', *BuzzFeed*, 8 August 2014. Last viewed 12 Novmber 2024 <https://www.buzzfeed.com/emilyorley/the-brownface-controversy-surrounding-jonah-from-tonga>.

'Press esc to exit full screen' (written in response to Hannah Brontë's 'MI$$-EUPNEA') appeared in *Bleed Echo: Running Dog*, Bleed 2020: Biennial live event in the everyday digital presented by Arts House and Campbelltown Arts Centre, Sydney, July 2020.

'for•te' appeared in *Forever Fresh Talanoa* series by Afatasi The Artist and Momoe i manu ae ala atea's Tasker, Contemporary Hum and In*ter*is*land Collective, Whangārei Aotearoa/New Zealand, February 2021.

'(Two of) the Bodies I Have Found' appeared in *Lua: A whole new world*, issue 2, *Tupuranga Journal*, Whangārei Aotearoa/New Zealand, April 2022.

'Our Mums' appeared in *Forever Fresh Talanoa* series by Afatasi The Artist and Momoe i manu ae ala atea's Tasker, Contemporary Hum and In*ter*is*land Collective, Whangārei Aotearoa/New Zealand, February 2021.

'fresh font' appeared in *Forever Fresh Talanoa* series by Afatasi The Artist and Momoe i manu ae ala atea's Tasker, Contemporary Hum and In*ter*is*land Collective, Whangārei Aotearoa/New Zealand, February 2021.

'Lion's Honey – A Reader's Moments' appeared in 'do it (australia)', Project 36, Kaldor Public Art Projects, Sydney, June 2020.

Words of Thanks

I thank the many lands that have held me whilst the vast imaginings and drafts, conversations and edits of these pages have been drawn, and I especially acknowledge the unceded lands of the Wangal, Gadigal, Dharawal, Meanjin and Bundjalung peoples of so-called Australia. I mihi to the tangata whenua of Aotearoa – in-particular dear ones in Hokianga, Te Whanganui-a-Tara and Tāmaki Makaurau – where I wrote some of my favourite poems for *Mettle.* Ngā mihi to the custodians of these ancient lands, whose moon and sun will forever light my poetic path.

Thank you to my mentors and friends, my writerly rocks – Natalie Harkin and Tony Birch – whose guidance and belief in my practice has been transformative.

I treasure the support I have received over the years from poetic tall-trees Joy Harjo, Ali Cobby Eckermann, Leanne Betasamosake Simpson, Tusiata Avia, Sandra Cisneros and Eve L. Ewing. Knowing each of you and learning from you completely crushed the myth that we should not meet our (s)heroes.

Several poems housed in *Mettle* emerged in 2019 when I studied a Māori and Pasifika Creative Writing subject at Victoria University in Wellington, led by the legendary Victor Roger. I am grateful to my fellow classmates who offered their insightful feedback and provided a nourishing community, allowing me to share new work freely. This rōpū helped anchor my voice and lay strong foundations for *Mettle.*

Ngā mihi to my takatāpui chosen whānau including my editor, essa may ranapiri, as well as Tessa Rose, Michaela Keeble, Alison Whittaker, Raelee Lancaster, Daniella

Trimboli and Jazz Money. There are too many other dear people to name here, but I'm sure you know who you are.

I am grateful to the editors and organisations who provided invaluable scaffolding and opportunities to create and mould many pieces within *Mettle*, including The In*ter*is*land Collective, *Tupuranga Journal* (including Jacqueline Carter) and The Next Chapter Fellowship (plus The Next Chapter Alumni Poetry Fellowship) at The Wheeler Centre.

Many thanks to the UQP team, especially Aviva Tuffield whose staunch support for Palestine and the Summer Reading for MPs project is an imperative and visionary action in the literary industry.

Thank you to Creative Australia for the vital funding, which allowed me to realise *Mettle* as a collection. Also thank you to Create NSW for supporting residencies including Varuna Writers House, Bundanon Artist Residency and Unyoked Residency.

Thank you to the extraordinarily talented Momoe i manu ae ala atea'e Tasker (my sis) for agreeing to create the *Mettle* cover art.

Sincere thanks to those who gave their precious energy and time to write generous words of endorsement for *Mettle,* including Aziembry Aolini (my g), Robert Sullivan (my whanaunga), Maarama Kāmira (my cuz), Daley Rangi (e hoa), essa may ranapiri (my baddie), Jazz Money, Natalie Harkin, Sandra Cisneros and Leanne Betasamosake Simpson. Each of these writers has their own extraordinary collections / books / works and I encourage you to go seek them out immediately.

A thread in *Mettle* I feel bittersweet about is that one of my brothers, Gerard, is no longer in this realm to share this pukapuka with. Gerry's quiet and unwavering support of my writing meant the world to me, and I feel very lucky that he patiently listened to me read many of the poems to him on the phone, before he passed away in February 2024. I'll never forget his response after reading him 'Blood Brothers' during a FaceTime chat. His giant smile and watery blue eyes cheekily glistened back at me, knowing that the poem featured him. I also treasure my dear Mum and Dad in their passings, and I thank them for instilling in me a deep love of reading and books. I am immensely grateful to my two remaining brothers, Damien and Sean, for their support. I'm also extremely grateful to Aunty Gayle and dear cousins Marie and Judy for their aroha.

Finally, sharing a key lesson learnt whilst writing these poems over the years; we develop mettle and strength by leaning into soft resilience and radical love – sources of true grit.